Truth
Is |
Power !

P. A. T.

P.A.T.

God Reveals a Mystery!

✦

Patricia A. Thomas

iUniverse, Inc.
New York   Bloomington

God Reveals a Mystery!

iUniverse books may be ordered through booksellers or by contacting:

iUniverse
1663 Liberty Drive
Bloomington, IN 47403
www.iuniverse.com
1-800-Authors (1-800-288-4677)

Because of the dynamic nature of the Internet, any Web addresses or links contained in this book may have changed since publication and may no longer be valid. The views expressed in this work are solely those of the author and do not necessarily reflect the views of the publisher, and the publisher hereby disclaims any responsibility for them.

ISBN: 978-0-595-40221-2 (pbk)
ISBN: 978-0-595-84597-2 (ebk)

Printed in the United States of America

Contents

Acknowledgements

I would first like to thank God, my Father, the Holy Spirit who leads me into all truth, and Jesus Christ, my Lord and Savior, for their love and for entrusting to me some of their great revelations. I would also like to thank my dear family, both biological and spiritual, for all of their love, support, and encouragement to know that God is with me, and for understanding the work that God has chosen me to do in the prophetic ministry called Words of Vision, because those without a vision will perish (Proverbs 29:18).

This book is dedicated to my beautiful and wise daughter, Patrice. I thank God that he could be so generous to give me such a wonderful blessing to have in my life! I love you!

Also, this book is dedicated to my Holy Bible study partner, my dear mother, Frankie Mae, whose unselfish love, hard work, and dedication to her three children can never be matched. Thank you so much for being the best mother in the world! I praise and thank God for giving you the strength to deliver me, a ten pound baby, into the world. I love you!

Finally, I would like to thank my maternal grandmother, Darleaner (Big Mama), who is now present with the Lord, for taking me to weekly Holy Bible study meetings as a child, and for taking me on fishing trips. I have grown from fishing for fish to fishing for men for Christ Jesus! I love you!

For nothing is secret that will not be revealed, nor *anything* hidden that will not be known and come to light. (Luke 8:17)

Introduction

Do you know the true origin of the devil? Does Satan have a God-given will or soul? Is Satan a cherub? Is Satan the fallen angel named Lucifer, who was once the director of the heavenly choir? Or is Satan a crafty serpent that tempted Adam and Eve in the Garden of Eden? Many things have been said about Satan, our enemy, which have become distorted pieces of a puzzle. God is going to sort out the pieces of this puzzle, and he will make a perfectly clear picture that will reveal Satan's true origin.

Sometimes the truth can be right in front of our faces, but if God doesn't want us to see it, we never will. The only way I am able to write about this great mystery, is because God opened my spiritual eyes and mind and allowed me to see the complete picture some years ago. I was young in the faith when God gave me an understanding of Satan's true origin, but Jesus tells us that God finds pleasure in doing that:

> At that time Jesus answered and said, "I thank You, Father, Lord of heaven and earth, that You have hidden these things from the wise and prudent and have revealed them to babes. Even so, Father, for so it seemed good in Your sight." (Matthew 11:25–26)

When I first received this information from God, I shared some of the information with some people to see if they knew about it, and they didn't. Even now there are many people of all ages and backgrounds who still don't know the true origin of Satan. God allowed me to know that he had a perfect plan in place to share this important knowledge, and it starts with me writing this book.

As a chosen prophetess and servant of God, I have the gift to see some of the future that God has planned. God has revealed to me that he will complete this puzzle to give people a biblical understanding of this profound mystery. As it says in the Holy Bible, "Surely the Lord GOD does nothing, Unless He reveals His secret to His servants the prophets" (Amos 3:7).

At times, some puzzles can have unnecessary pieces that need to be discarded. For the puzzle of Satan's true origin, we must remove two pieces that have commonly been misused: the fallen angel named Lucifer and the cherub. The discussion of these popular false identities of Satan will shine the light on an area of darkness and confusion.

Next, we can start putting this puzzle together by examining the few pieces that are needed to understand this mystery. The first necessary piece is the Holy Bible. God wants each of us to re-examine what the Holy Bible says about our enemy, the devil. The devil has been misidentified for centuries by many to be something other than what God created him to be on the sixth day of Creation. It is time for all of us to be aware of the true beginning of our biggest adversary. I am going to examine the same holy scriptures that many of us are familiar with, but with God's knowledge and understanding. It is my hope and prayer that my book will allow many to read the Holy Bible and pay closer attention to every word, letter, comma, and period. And, if we don't understand something, to pray to God for counseling and understanding. God has His word here for us to read it and not to ignore it. The Holy Bible is the best book ever written, and because of the technology that is available to us, there is no reason for anyone to ignore it. We must all study the Holy Bible and be approved by God's standards.

> Be diligent to present yourself approved to God, a worker
> who does not need to be ashamed, rightly dividing the word
> of truth. (2 Timothy 2:15)

The next piece of the puzzle is the serpent. Around the world, the serpent is depicted in its cursed form as it tempts Eve to eat the fruit of the tree of the knowledge of good and evil. However, according to the third chapter of Genesis, the serpent is not cursed to be on its belly until after it successfully tempts our original parents. So, we must find out, what form the serpent was in before it was cursed.

The next two pieces of the puzzle of Satan's true origin are the dinosaur and the dragon. The dragon has been mistakenly called the dinosaur. The word dinosaur is a made-up name for fossils that are truly dragons. This name was given to the fossils because dragons are not supposed to have lived here on earth. The name dinosaur (dinosauria), which means "terrible lizard" in Greek, was coined for these fossils around 1842 because this animal was unknown at the time, by those who discovered them. Many take it as a fact that the name dinosaur is the animal's original name, but it isn't. Adam, who was the first man, named all of the livestock, birds of the air, and beasts of the field (Genesis 2:19-20). The Holy Bible mentions all types of animals such as the eagle, the lion, and the sheep, and it would be odd if it did not to talk about the dragon, whose fossils have been found in many places on the earth. The truth of the matter is that God does talk about the animals that became these fossils in great detail using this animal's Adam-given name.

The name of dragon, which means serpent in Greek, has been around for thousands of years, and both the names "dragon" and "serpent" are recorded in the Holy Bible. Those who live on and are from the continent of Asia (primarily the country of China) are especially adamant about the dragon.

Unfortunately, various barriers have kept many from agreeing about the true identity of this animal's fossils. Many facts have been mixed with fiction, which has distorted the image of the true animal referred to with the false name of the dinosaur. The true animal is the dragon, and it is not a fabled animal as told in fairy tales. Many people do know that dinosaurs are really dragons. People have talked about and created the dragons' images long before the dinosaurs were invented by misguided thoughts. But, this begs the question: What really happened to the dragons? There has to be an answer out there somewhere, and only in the Holy Bible will you find the true answer.

The final and most important piece to this puzzle is God. Only God can reveal the answer to us in simple terms. Please keep in mind that God has no limits, and he can do anything. If you don't have that perception, then this may be difficult to believe. So many things have been said and written that, we have allowed our minds to accept information that is widespread, even though it is not true. Again, God can do anything. With this on your mind, while reading my book, you will be able to sift out some of those distorted theories that have built up in your mind about the dinosaur. The dinosaur is the mythical creature, not the real dragon. The dragon, in a different form, still roams the earth. The dragon is not extinct.

God's answer will put the final piece in the puzzle of the real origin of Satan. Only God knows everything. It doesn't matter where or how you dig for the fossils. What matters is who left the fossils behind to tell the story. Only God is able to give us the true story of what happened to this animal because He was there. Without God, it would be impossible to tell what happened to this mystifying animal that Adam named as serpent or dragon.

With my book, I will dispel only some of the lies, myths, and fallacies that have kept so many of us from knowing the true origin of Satan. Many things have become confusing about the devil's true origin, and many people around the world teach about and preach against Satan without knowing his true origin or identity. But God will open the door for the truth to be told, if we ask, seek, and knock:

> "Ask, and it will be given to you; seek, and you will find; knock, and it will be opened to you. For everyone who asks receives, and he who seeks finds, and to him who knocks it will be opened." (Matthew 7:7-8)

My book's sole purpose is not to entertain anyone, but to enlighten everyone. There will be no fancy words in my book as I deliver the answer to this "great mystery." We all must continue to grow in the truth, and simplicity is the best way to deliver information to people. My opening chapter starts the process of putting the correct pieces together to this puzzle that has mystified many. It is my hope and prayer that my short and to-the-point book will open the spiritual eyes and minds for many to see a perfectly clear picture, just as God has allowed me to see it.

1
Revealing the Tempter

The Forbidden Tree: The Taste of Death

Now the serpent was more cunning than any beast of the field which the Lord God had made. And he said to the woman, "Has God indeed said, 'You shall not eat of every tree of the garden'?" And the woman said to the serpent, "We may eat the fruit of the trees of the garden; but of the fruit of the tree which is in the midst of the garden, God has said, 'You shall not eat it, nor shall you touch it, lest you die.'" Then the serpent said to the woman, "You will not surely die. For God knows that in the day you eat of it your eyes will be opened, and you will be like God, knowing good and evil." So when the woman saw that the tree was good for food, that it was pleasant to the eyes, and a tree desirable to make one wise, she took of its fruit and ate. She also gave to her husband with her, and he ate. Then the eyes of both of them were opened, and they knew that they were naked; and they sewed fig leaves together and made themselves coverings. (Genesis 3:1-7)

This scripture passages shows the beginning of Adam and Eve's fall, which resulted from the serpent's, or dragon's, temptation. God had told Adam and Eve, however, that they were to have dominion over all the animals (Genesis 1:28). God made the serpent's, or the dragon's, spirit the most Satanic, so the serpent would be more cunning and more subtle than the livestock and wild animals, which was an existing condition. This allows us to know that God created the livestock and wild animals' spirits to be crafty, but God created the dragon's spirit to be craftier. The dragon never chose to be more cunning or more crafty; God chose to create the dragon that way for His purpose and will. The serpent and all other animals have spirits, but they do not have a God-given free will, or soul, like humans.

In this scripture from the book of Genesis, Adam and Eve had a desire to be like God, so the dragon could successfully tempt them. That is how our disobedient parents of the Garden of Eden failed. Because of Adam and Eve's failure to obey God, we are born into iniquity (Ephesians 2:1).

With this act of disobedience, they lost their home and were cast out of the beautiful Garden of Eden (Genesis 3:23). Being created in the image of God is awesome enough, but Adam and Eve desired to have God's knowledge of both good and evil. When they became aware of good and evil, Adam and Eve became responsible for their actions. If they would not have eaten the forbidden fruit, they could have done both good and evil deeds, but they would not have been held accountable. In addition, they would have, remained innocent, and would not have died. However, with this tempting desire to know the difference between good and evil, the forbidden fruit was their taste of death.

God, who is perfect, created a tree that had both good and evil knowledge in its fruit to test Adam and Eve. Again, the knowledge of evil was present in the fruit. As stated before, God created the dragon to be more cunning and crafty than other animals. God made these animals this way for His purpose and plan. No one should question God's wisdom, His divine plan, or His ways. God allows us to know in the book of Isaiah that he is above our ways, thoughts, and understanding: "For my thoughts are not your thoughts, nor are your ways my ways," says the Lord. "For as the heavens are higher than the earth, so are my ways higher than your ways, and my thoughts than your thoughts" (Isaiah 55:8-9).

The conversation that the dragon had with Eve in Genesis 3:1-5 was normal. The dragon talked to Eve, and Eve talked back to the animal with ease. After the curse, animals were no longer able to talk. As evidence that animals could talk, God has left the parrot, which mimics some words that it hears but has no ability to converse with humans.

> And he was given a mouth speaking great things and blasphemies, and he was given authority to continue for forty-two months. Then he opened his mouth in blasphemy against God, to blaspheme His name, His tabernacle, and those who dwell in heaven. (Revelation 13:5–6)

> Then I saw another beast coming up out of the earth, and he had two horns like a lamb and spoke like a dragon. And

he exercises all the authority of the first beast in his presence, and causes the earth and those who dwell in it to worship the first beast, whose deadly wound was healed. He performs great signs, so that he even makes fire come down from heaven on the earth in the sight of men. And he deceives those who dwell on the earth by those signs which he was granted to do in the sight of the beast, telling those who dwell on the earth to make an image to the beast who was wounded by the sword and lived. (Revelation 13:11-14)

These passages from the book of Revelation, once again, indicate that animals or beasts will be given the ability to speak. Just like the dragon, or serpent, who used his mouth in Genesis to lie about God and to tempt Eve to contradict His command to not eat from the forbidden tree, these beasts will be given the ability to speak for the purpose of God's will to be done during the time of the apocalypse. These two beasts will say blasphemous things against God, His dwelling place, and those who live in heaven. These beasts will boast about the dragon, which is the devil. Later, the apostle John writes that the spirits of frogs (animals) will come out of the beasts' mouths (Revelation 16:13). These beasts will make war against the saints, and they will tempt man about what God has commanded by His holy word. The Holy Bible makes it perfectly clear that no one will be like the beast that Satan gave power to, and no one will be able to make war against it (Revelation 13:4). Why? Because he will not be a man but a beast with power and authority (Revelation 13:2). These passages do not use these beasts as a metaphor for something or someone else. These two beasts will actually be beasts, as the Holy Bible literally and simply describes them.

In the Holy Bible, when God gives someone a dream or a vision with symbols and metaphors, an interpretation follows at God's appointed time. For example, Joseph interprets Pharaoh's dream in Genesis chapter 41, and the angel Gabriel interprets Daniel's dream and vision in Daniel chapters 7 and 8. Therefore, these beasts are not symbols of something or someone else. There is no need for God to give an interpretation or an explanation because these beasts will be literal animals. The apostle John never wrote an interpretation of the beasts because it wasn't necessary. In Genesis 1:20 and 1:24, the sea and earth brought forth the animals, and in Revelation 13:1 and 13:11, once again the sea and earth will bring forth animals or beasts.

Apostle Paul writes that it was a crafty serpent/dragon that successfully tempted Eve (2 Corinthians 11:3). It may be difficult for some to accept that an animal tricked our original parents because God gave, Adam and Eve dominion over all animals, and he commanded Adam and Eve to subdue them. However, in the books of Genesis and Revelation, we see that animals or beasts are being used to deceive humans. Many people do allow and have allowed animals to be their gods. Anything that you worship, such as money, is your god. That is why God commands us not to place anyone or anything above him (Exodus 20:3). God also warns us not to make idols or images to worship (Exodus 20:4-5). Nevertheless, rebellious people worshipping animals and making idol statues, or images, of animals are shown in these passages from Exodus and Revelation:

> So all the people broke off the golden earrings which were in their ears, and brought them to Aaron. And he received the gold from their hand, and he fashioned it with an engraving tool, and made a molded calf. Then they said, "This is your god, O Israel, that brought you out of the land of Egypt!" (Exodus 32: 3-4)

> And he deceives those who dwell on the earth by those signs which he was granted to do in the sight of the beast, telling those who dwell on the earth to make an image to the beast who was wounded by the sword and lived. (Revelation 13:14)

There are things that are written in the book of Revelation that we have never witnessed before. Some of those unknown things are hail and fire mixed with blood, which cause a third of the trees and all of the grass to burn up (Revelation 8:7). Another scripture in Revelation tells us that locusts will be shaped like horses with men's faces, women's hair, and will have lion's teeth (Revelation 9:7-8). It also plainly tells us that the first beast's image (statue or idol) will come to life and will be able to speak (Revelation 13:15). There are other horrific things that will take place on earth during the apocalypse. Therefore, it shouldn't be inconceivable that beasts will be able to talk and perform miraculous signs (Revelation 16:3) and one will speak like a dragon (Revelation 13:11), not like a man. Especially since the Holy Bible states just that. We must always understand that God, who is unlimited, can and does give us information that does not need to be interpreted or translated. With that said, some have stated that a third of the stars written in Revelation 12:4, that the dragon's tail swept to the earth, are making a reference to angels, but the scripture does not tell us that. Let us closely examine this scripture:

> His tail drew a third of the stars of heaven and threw them to the earth. And the dragon stood before the woman who was ready to give birth, to devour her Child as soon as it was born. (Revelation 12:4)

Concerning stars, let us take note that there are interpretations in Revelation 1:20 that allow us to know that the seven stars represent the angels of the seven churches and in Genesis 37: 9-11, Joseph's dream of the eleven stars bowing down to him represent his 11 brothers.

The Curse: The Fall Was Great!

So the Lord God said to the serpent: "Because you have done this, You are cursed more than all cattle, And more than every beast of the field; On your belly you shall go, And you shall eat dust All the days of your life. And I will put enmity between you and the woman, And between your seed and her Seed; He shall bruise your head, And you shall bruise his heel." To the woman He said: "I will greatly multiply your sorrow and your conception; In pain you shall bring forth children; Your desire shall be for your husband, And he shall rule over you." Then to Adam He said, "Because you have heeded the voice of your wife, and have eaten from the tree of which I commanded you, saying, 'You shall not eat of it': "Cursed is the ground for your sake; In toil you shall eat of it All the days of your life. Both thorns and thistles it shall bring forth for you, And you shall eat the herb of the field. In the sweat of your face you shall eat bread Till you return to the ground, For out of it you were taken; For dust you are, and to dust you shall return." (Genesis 3:14-19)

This passage tells us that the serpent, or dragon, was cursed more than all livestock and wild animals in size; because this more crafty, or subtle, animal initially tempted Eve. After Eve was tempted, she gave some of the forbidden fruit to Adam, who was with her (Genesis 3:6). This event began our spiritual separation from God. The Lord God cursed the dragon to become a dust eater, which affected all dragons. The cunning devil's lie to Adam and Eve caused their downfall, but it also caused the dragon's downfall. God punished the dragon, which had no will, for its lie by cursing it to become what we commonly know today as the snake. God cursed the dragon because that was His will.

Many pictures from around the world portray the serpent in its cursed form, on its belly, as it tempts Eve. This depiction is incorrect because the scripture says clearly that the serpent's form was larger than the form of a snake that has no limbs when it initiated the conversation of deceit with Eve. According to God's truthful word, the serpent, or dragon, was not neither possessed by another spiritual being, nor was it disguised to tempt Eve and Adam. It looked like an animal, and it was an animal with a devious spirit, just as God created it.

What does Genesis 3:14 reveal? It reveals to us that God's power is infinite, and that he can create an animal and make its fall great to become that same animal, that becomes a lowly animal, with the command of His powerful voice.

The curses that God placed on Adam and Eve in Genesis 3:15–19, for their original act of disobedience affect all of us today. The curse that God placed on the serpents (dragons) was greater than the other animals'. God's curses were like a domino effect that affects all of mankind, all serpents or dragons, and all animals on the face of the earth. Even though we are under a curse, we who believe in Jesus Christ are awaiting the day to be regenerated from our corruptible bodies to incorruptible bodies:

> For we know that the whole creation groans and labors with birth pangs together until now. Not only that, but we also who have the first fruits of the Spirit, even we ourselves groan within ourselves, eagerly waiting for the adoption, the redemption of our body. (Romans 8:22-23)

> And He said to them, "I saw Satan fall like lightning from heaven. Behold, I give you the authority to trample on serpents and scorpions, and over all the power of the enemy, and nothing shall by any means hurt you. Nevertheless do not rejoice in this, that the spirits are subject to you, but rather rejoice because your names are written in heaven." (Luke 10:18-20)

In this passage from the New Testament, Jesus wisely tells us that the serpent, dragon, or Satan, which had the ability to fly, came down "like lightning from heaven" because of the curse. Jesus witnessed Satan's, or the dragon's, fall. Some were on the land, in water, and others were flying in the sky, and they fell to the ground instantly after God spoke the curse. With

Jesus' use of the word "heaven" in this passage, we must know that he was not referring to third heaven, where God resides (2 Corinthians 12:2), nor second heaven, but first heaven, which includes the sky where some animals fly (Genesis 1:8).

The next verse of Luke 10 parallels Genesis 3:15. Jesus allows us to clearly understand that is why we now have the authority to trample on, or crush, spiritual serpents, spiritual scorpions, and all of the powers of the enemy, which are our foes, and they will not harm us. The enmity that God placed between us and Satan puts all of us in constant battle with him and his demons. Satan, who can strike our heels, has these powers by God's permission, which is stated in Genesis 3:15. However, with Christ Jesus, we are greater than any powers that the devil has. As Jesus says in 1 John 4:4, "You are of God, little children, and have overcome them, because He who is in you is greater than he who is in the world."

Jesus mentions serpents and scorpions in the same context because that is the existence or being of spiritual Satan. Jesus never said Satan fell like lightning as an angel of light who was rebellious. Jesus plainly tells us that, by His authority, spiritual Satan, serpents, scorpions, and other evil powers can be conquered. Powerful Jesus did cast out demons (Matthew 17:18), and he told us that we would be able to do greater works than him (John 14:12). Those who have been given the power to cast out demons have witnessed spiritual serpents, scorpions, spiders, and other wicked spirits coming out of people possessed by demons. People witness these wicked spirits because that is what they physically used to be. As a prophetess of God, I have been given the gift to see both good and evil things in the spiritual realm. I have seen serpents, scorpions, spiders, and other forms of spirits that the enemy uses, which are part of his evil powers.

The Proof: The Dragons' Fossils Left Behind

> In the six hundredth year of Noah's life, in the second month, the seventeenth day of the month, on that day all the fountains of the great deep were broken up, and the windows of heaven were opened. And the rain was on the earth forty days and forty nights. (Genesis 7:11-12)

> And it came to pass in the six hundred and first year, in the first month, the first day of the month, that the waters were dried up from the earth; and Noah removed the covering of the ark and looked, and indeed the surface of the ground was dry. And in the second month, on the twenty-seventh day of the month, the earth was dried. (Genesis 8:13-14)

Although waters from the deep came forth during the great flood, God did not destroy the ground or the land. God secured the dragons' fossils in the ground for His divine purpose. The land eventually dried, and Noah and his family were able to walk on it again. The fossils God left behind are proof that what he said is true. The serpent's, or dragon's, fossils are evidence that it existed as an animal larger than a snake. The dragon had more bones than the cursed snake, or the new serpent. The extra bones and flesh were removed by God when he cursed the dragon, which made it lose its original identity.

After a time, these extra bones that were left on the ground because of the curse became fossilized, or embedded in the earth's crust. The foreknowledge allowed him to keep the fossils safe to prove that the curse of the dragon did take place, and that the bones belonged to the spiritual devil, or Satan.

The exact dates for the curse of man and serpent and the great flood are not recorded in the holy scriptures. However, God does record the genealogical line from Adam to Noah and each descendant's age in Genesis chapter 5. Therefore, by reading, we can see that centuries are between Adam and Noah, which gives the bones ample time after the curse of the dragon to be embedded in the earth's crust. Noah was six hundred years old when the great flood occurred (Genesis 7:6). Some have mistakenly stated that the dragon, in its original form, was aboard Noah's ark. However, that is inaccurate because the curse of the dragon, or serpent, took place before the great flood. The cursed serpent and other animals were on Noah's ark, as detailed in the following holy verses:

> And of every living thing of all flesh you shall bring two of every sort into the ark, to keep them alive with you; they shall be male and female. Of the birds after their kind, of animals after their kind, and of every creeping thing of the earth after its kind, two of every kind will come to you to keep them alive. (Genesis 6:19-20)

Dragon (Old Serpent) or Dinosaur?

So the great dragon was cast out, that serpent of old, called the Devil and Satan, who deceives the whole world; he was cast to the earth, and his angels were cast out with him. (Revelation 12:9)

He laid hold of the dragon, that serpent of old, who is the Devil and Satan, and bound him for a thousand years; (Revelation 20:2)

The words dragon, serpent of old, devil, and Satan are synonymous in these two verses in the book of Revelation. These words are imperative to reveal the serpent's original form, and the apostle John wisely uses them to give us a better understanding that they are all the same.

Let me first focus on serpent of old and dragon. The old and new serpents were in the Old World (before and after the curse), because when God spoke to it, he said to him, "Serpent." The old serpent represents the ancient serpent, just like the Old World represents the Ancient World. The old also represents the former in both cases. The word serpent was what God called this animal, in its initial form, but the term old, as used by the wise apostle John in the book of Revelation, referred to how this animal used to be as the larger dragon with limbs. God did not say "old serpent" to it before the curse because, it was only in the state of the fully formed dragon.

Now, I will examine the words Satan and devil. The most misguided identity in the Holy Bible, is how Satan or the devil looked when it tempted Eve. As mentioned before, the wicked spirit of Satan is the wicked spirit of the dragon. The spiritual entity of the devil, which means slanderer in Greek, is part of the crafty, or cunning, dragon's character. The Holy Bible, if interpreted correctly, never refers to the devil as anything but an animal, which God created on the sixth day. The Holy Bible makes no statement, that Satan camouflaged or disguised itself, or tried to conceal its true identity when it spoke to Eve. The dragon or serpent's character in the Bible always has a crafty, cunning, or devious spirit by God's design. Therefore, the holy scriptures are not misleading because the spirit of Satan did not disguise itself to be a dragon. The dragon's spirit was the devil.

The Holy Bible is always right, and it is impossible for God to lie. There was no disguise. God spoke to and cursed the actual animal, the dragon. If it was anything other than an animal, why doesn't the Bible state that? Throughout the Holy Bible, the scriptures consistently show the devil as a serpent or dragon. The words serpent and dragon are interchangeably used in God's word because they mean the same thing. Even God himself describes the serpent, or Satan, in His holy word. By reading further in my book, you will see some of the scriptures I have chosen will reflect that.

Now that the picture has been accurately repainted to reveal the true animal in the beautiful Garden of Eden, we can see that the dinosaur wasn't that animal. Because this animal was renamed, its identity has confused many people. With God's perfect timing, he makes us aware that he wants us to know now. Because some people do not always seek out God first for answers, the dragon has been portrayed as a boring-colored dinosaur creature with many names attached to it. It has become the frightful, mysterious, flesh-eating creature incorrectly depicted in art, movies, books, toys, and in other places. But, dragons, the true animals, were beautiful in color, and the snakes you see today have the same colorings as dragons once did. With that being said about the external look of the dragon, with many of the fossil findings, limited bones have been found which has allowed some people to guess, assume, or make-up what the internal structure is beyond the dragon. No one should assume how an animal looked if many of the bones are missing. We need proof and the bones need to be available to see an accurate description of these animals' internal structure.

The name dinosaur was coined because some people simply didn't know that the fossils that were found throughout the earth are really dragons. As mentioned before, some people do know that the discovered fossils are dragons. Unfortunately, over time facts have become distorted, but if you do limited research about the dinosaur, you will find out that it is not the true name of that animal. Instead of researching for ourselves, some of us have allowed the facts to be mixed with fiction. But, thank God that His will is for the true animal to be revealed!

One of the fictitious or false points that is circulating about the dinosaurs is that they dwelled on the earth millions of years ago. However, the Holy Bible has genealogical records and other information that allows us to know that the earth is less than six thousand years old. The earth was void in Genesis 1:2, and the earth was formed out of water in 2 Peter 3:5.

Other falsehoods about the demise of the dinosaur are major catastrophes, such as a global volcanic eruption and large meteors impacting earth. God's simple answer is that the dragons are not extinct, but they are cursed.

2

God: The Author of Creation

In the Beginning: The Sixth Day of Creation

Then God said, "Let the earth bring forth the living creature according to its kind: cattle and creeping thing and beast of the earth, each according to its kind"; and it was so. And God made the beast of the earth according to its kind, cattle according to its kind, and everything that creeps on the earth according to its kind. And God saw that it was good. Then God said, "Let Us make man in Our image, according to Our likeness; let them have dominion over the fish of the sea, over the birds of the air, and over the cattle, over all the earth and over every creeping thing that creeps on the earth." So God created man in His own image; in the image of God He created him; male and female He created them. Then God blessed them, and God said to them, "Be fruitful and multiply; fill the earth and subdue it; have dominion over the fish of the sea, over the birds of the air, and over every living thing that moves on the earth." (Genesis 1:24-28)

Then God saw everything that He had made, and indeed it was very good. So the evening and the morning were the sixth day. (Genesis 1:31)

In these scriptures, it is important to note that God created the serpent and its craftiness on the sixth day before he created man. We both come from the earth, or the dust of the ground, and we have co-existed since the sixth day of Creation. The holy scriptures speak for themselves, and they say that the serpent was just an animal. The serpent, or dragon, is a wild animal of the field. God will completely destroy the lies and misconceptions of what the serpent looked like. The lies will soon be exposed by God's glorious light. The devil has always brought distortion and lies to conceal what is the godly truth.

What Did They Eat?

Then God said, "Let the earth bring forth the living creature according to its kind: cattle and creeping thing and beast of the earth, each according to its kind"; and it was so. And God made the beast of the earth according to its kind, cattle according to its kind, and everything that creeps on the earth according to its kind. And God saw that it was good. Then God said, "Let Us make man in Our image, according to Our likeness; let them have dominion over the fish of the sea, over the birds of the air, and over the cattle, over all the earth and over every creeping thing that creeps on the earth." So God created man in His own image; in the image of God He created him; male and female He created them. Then God blessed them, and God said to them, "Be fruitful and multiply; fill the earth and subdue it; have dominion over the fish of the sea, over the birds of the air, and over every living thing that moves on the earth." And God said, "See, I have given you every herb that yields seed which is on the face of all the earth, and every tree whose fruit yields seed; to you it shall be for food. Also, to every beast of the earth, to every bird of the air, and to everything that creeps on the earth, in which there is life, I have given every green herb for food"; and it was so. (Genesis 1:24-30)

Many untruths surround the mythical dinosaurs' eating habits, some of which say some dinosaurs were carnivores. However, in the true beginning, all livings things, including dragons, ate plants as God commanded. The seed-bearing plants were for humans, and the green plants were for animals. At this time, no person or animal was a carnivore. They were all plants eaters, or herbivores. In the beginning, plants were the only source of food for them. God can't lie, and if he commanded all beings to only eat plants, then that is all they ate. According to God's command and word, carnivores, or any flesh eaters, were not present during the beginning of Creation.

Since God put the dragon, or old serpent, on its belly after the curse, it never got a chance to be a carnivore in its original state. However, today most snakes are flesh-eating reptiles. After the great flood, God allowed Noah and his family to eat animals with no life blood in them, and he allowed the animals to be carnivores too (Genesis 9:3-4).

How Did They Live Together?

> Then God saw everything that He had made, and indeed it was very good. So the evening and the morning were the sixth day. (Genesis 1:31)

The key words in this verse are "very good." The Garden of Eden was a beautiful paradise for man and animal. It was a glorious beginning for all living things! Everything that God had created during days one through six were pleasing to him according to His perfect will and plan. Unlike some of the lies of man and animal's co-existence on the earth, as being disorderly, God's answer does not reflect what some have erroneously assumed.

Everything could have been done in a second, but it allowed God to establish time for man, and to establish the seventh day as His holy day of resting from His work that he had created (Genesis 2:3). God, who has no beginning of days or end of days, has lived forever and doesn't need time.

3

Evil Is in the Devil

The Devil Is a Liar!

> You are of your father the devil, and the desires of your father you want to do. He was a murderer from the beginning, and does not stand in the truth, because there is no truth in him. When he speaks a lie, he speaks from his own resources, for he is a liar and the father of it. (John 8:44)

This passage shows that Jesus didn't say the words "before the beginning he was a murderer and does not stand in the truth." Jesus carefully states, "from the beginning he was a murderer and does not stand in the truth." This means that from the sixth day of Creation Satan was a murderer and a liar. As already mentioned, the devil or dragon was created on the sixth day, and then man also was created on that same day. Man's perceived image of the devil is one the biggest misconceptions of all. The spiritual devil, or Satan, is an enemy to mankind. His venomous tongue has made many become easy prey for him. In order to know what is against you, shouldn't you find out who your enemy truly is first? The devil is a liar! The devil, the master of deception, deceives the whole world (Revelation 12:9). Therefore, God commands us not to be a part of the deceptive and evil world, but to be transformed by renewing our minds through Christ Jesus (Romans 12:2).

> For such are false apostles, deceitful workers, transforming themselves into apostles of Christ. And no wonder! For Satan himself transforms himself into an angel of light. (2 Corinthians 11:13-14)

The word angel simply means "messenger" in Greek. There are two types of spiritual messengers: God's messengers of light, and Satan's messengers of darkness, which are demons and both types of messengers were created by God. The Holy Bible never states that Satan was an angel of God, and Satan never will be a true angel of light. The archangel Michael and the angel Gabriel are messengers of God, or of light, as mentioned in Jude 1:9 and Luke 1:26. The devil transforms into, masquerades as, or pretends to be an angel of light in order to trick us to believe something that looks and sounds good, but is actually evil. God's word wisely describes the character of His true angels of light:

> "And of the angels He says: 'Who makes His angels spirits And His ministers a flame of fire'" (Hebrews 1:7). God's word also says, "Are they not all ministering spirits sent forth to minister for those who will inherit salvation?" (Hebrews 1:14).

Halloween is a day that originates from Satan's deceiving ways. It attempts to wean out the hallowed ("Hallowed be Thy name" (Matthew 6:9)), and allows those who participate in this event, to be something they are not. That is how the devil, false apostles, false prophets, false evangelists, false pastors, false teachers, and other deceitful workers of wickedness always use distortion and lies to conceal the godly truth. The devil wants this illusion of being something that he is not to continue. Satan has mischievously preyed on us because many of us have misidentified him. But God, who is faithful, always shines a bright light on what is false, and he allows His true servants to spread the word of truth! In these times of great deception, we must pray, watch, and always be discerning, as Peter states, "But the end of all things is at hand; therefore be serious and watchful in your prayers" (1 Peter 4:7).

There is no coincidence that the word evil is in the devil's name. At times, God makes things so obvious, but many just choose to ignore them. Many people misidentify the devil in the following ways: as a heavenly being that was formerly the director of the heavenly choir, or as a player of instruments, or has instruments coming out of it, or as a being that was here before God created the heavens and the earth, or as an archangel, or as the destroyer of a previous earth. He has also been misidentified in innumerable other ways. There are so many false statements out there that have been passed down for many years. None of these statements coincides with the identity of the devil in holy biblical scriptures, and the Holy Bible has the final say and authority in all matters. God is infallible, and His truthful word will always stand and prove that.

> But He, knowing their thoughts, said to them: "Every
> kingdom divided against itself is brought to desolation, and
> a house divided against a house falls. If Satan also is divided
> against himself, how will his kingdom stand? Because
> you say I cast out demons by Beelzebub. And if I cast out
> demons by Beelzebub, by whom do your sons cast them
> out? Therefore they will be your judges. (Luke 11:17-19)

Jesus allows us to understand in the book of Luke that Beelzebub is another alias for the devil. He also says that spiritual Satan does conquer and divide, but he wouldn't divide and conquer his own spiritual kingdom of darkness and wickedness. He wants to keep it intact so he and his demons, or evil messengers, can continue to try to kill us, steal from us, and destroy us (John 10:10). But, thanks be to God's unselfish love that allowed Jesus to give us authority to trample on or crush the head of the devil, or snake! (Genesis 3:15, Luke 10:19)

The Holy Bible gives us some insight into Satan's spiritual kingdom of darkness in heaven. Daniel, who was in the earthly kingdom of Persia, received a vision that needed an interpretation in Daniel chapter 10. Therefore, an angel of light was sent to Daniel to give him an interpretation. However, Persia's spiritual kingdom of darkness hindered the angel of God for twenty-one days until the archangel Michael, called "chief prince" in this chapter, helped him. So, the geographical location of the earthly Persian Kingdom also has a wicked spiritual kingdom above it in heaven:

> Then he said to me, "Do not fear, Daniel, for from the first
> day that you set your heart to understand, and to humble
> yourself before your God, your words were heard; and I have
> come because of your words. But the prince of the kingdom
> of Persia withstood me twenty-one days; and behold,
> Michael, one of the chief princes, came to help me, for I
> had been left alone there with the kings of Persia. (Daniel
> 10:12-13)

Later, in the book of Revelation, there is a battle in heaven. The devil and his angels lose their kingdom in heaven after the fight against the archangel Michael and his angels of God. As a result, the devil and his demons, who roam the earth (Job 1:7), are thrown to the earth, which becomes their only place to dwell. The apostle John describes this battle:

> And war broke out in heaven: Michael and his angels fought
> with the dragon; and the dragon and his angels fought, but
> they did not prevail, nor was a place found for them in

heaven any longer. So the great dragon was cast out, that serpent of old, called the Devil and Satan, who deceives the whole world; he was cast to the earth, and his angels were cast out with him. (Revelation 12:7-9)

The Devil's False Identities: Angel of Light, Lucifer, and Cherub

> For if God did not spare the angels who sinned, but cast them down to hell and delivered them into chains of darkness, to be reserved for judgment; (2 Peter 2:4)

> And the angels who did not keep their proper domain, but left their own abode, He has reserved in everlasting chains under darkness for the judgment of the great day; (Jude 1:6)

These very important passages clearly tell us that all the free-willed, true, and original spiritual angels of God, who rebelled and abandoned their place of power, are eternally chained in a dark place waiting to be judged. Therefore, if they are chained, they can't move. The spiritual devil and his demons were never angels of light, but they are angels (messengers) of darkness. If they were, they wouldn't be present now causing havoc in our lives; they would be in chains awaiting judgment, too. God is in control. The Holy Bible, God's word, does not contradict itself. There are no rebellious angels of God roaming the earth or the heavens. With that said, the devil and his demons are loose and are moving around, which is stated in the book of Job: "And the Lord said to Satan, 'From where do you come?' So Satan answered the Lord and said, 'From going to and fro on the earth, and from walking back and forth on it'" (Job 1:7). The apostle Peter also wisely advises us: "Be sober, be vigilant; because your adversary the devil walks about like a roaring lion, seeking whom he may devour" (1 Peter 5:8).

Also, other scriptures allow us to understand that presently, the devil can move around, but he will be immobile when he is thrown into the bottomless pit, or abyss, sealed, and shut up during Jesus Christ's thousand-year reign, as shown below:

> Then I saw an angel coming down from heaven, having the key to the bottomless pit and a great chain in his hand. He laid hold of the dragon, that serpent of old, who is the Devil and Satan, and bound him for a thousand years; and he cast him into the bottomless pit, and shut him up, and set a seal on him, so that he should deceive the nations no more till the thousand years were finished. But after these things he must be released for a little while. (Revelation 20:13)

One of the most prominent misunderstandings of Satan's identity is found in the fourteenth chapter of Isaiah. It is imperative that we closely examine what God said through the Prophet Isaiah to know who God is talking about. Let us first look at these passages:

> It shall come to pass in the day the Lord gives you rest from your sorrow, and from your fear and the hard bondage in which you were made to serve, that you will take up this proverb against the king of Babylon, and say: "How the oppressor has ceased, The golden city ceased! The Lord has broken the staff of the wicked, The scepter of the rulers; He who struck the people in wrath with a continual stroke, He who ruled the nations in anger, Is persecuted and no one hinders. The whole earth is at rest and quiet; They break forth into singing. Indeed the cypress trees rejoice over you, And the cedars of Lebanon, Saying, 'Since you were cut down, No woodsman has come up against us.' (Isaiah 14:3-8)

In this passage from Isaiah, God mocks the prideful and tyrannical king of Babylon, "also known as the golden city," who conquered many nations. At this time, God's people, the Israelites, were being oppressed by the king of Babylon, and God allows Isaiah to know that their oppression and suffering would end. The Israelites' sin caused their oppression and suffering because God allowed them to be taken as captives by the Babylonians. But God promised that he would once again have mercy on them:

> For the Lord will have mercy on Jacob, and will still choose Israel, and settle them in their own land. The strangers will be joined with them, and they will cling to the house

of Jacob. Then people will take them and bring them to their place, and the house of Israel will possess them for servants and maids in the land of the Lord; they will take them captive whose captives they were, and rule over their oppressors. (Isaiah 14:1-2)

The next biblical reference speaks of the king of Babylon's impending death, and those who wait for him in hell to taunt him. These scriptures also indicate that the king of Babylon had servants who played stringed instruments for him. The fourteenth chapter of Isaiah never states that God is describing an angel, in which many are falsely stating that it is roaming the earth. God allows us to know that he is describing a man, because once the king of Babylon is in Sheol (with no ability to be on the earth), his flesh is covered with maggots and worms, as seen in these passages:

"Hell from beneath is excited about you, To meet you at your coming; It stirs up the dead for you, All the chief ones of the earth; It has raised up from their thrones All the kings of the nations. They all shall speak and say to you: 'Have you also become as weak as we? Have you become like us? Your pomp is brought down to Sheol, And the sound of your stringed instruments; The maggot is spread under you, And worms cover you.'" (Isaiah 14:9-11)

The pagan king of Babylon's self-glorified name was Lucifer, or "morning star." He was arrogant and assumed that he could ascend above God's holy throne. For this reason, God uses the king of Babylon's pompous words and turns them against the king to embarrass him. The fallen king could never ascend above God's holy throne, although he thought in his heart that he could. God would never allow it!

"How you are fallen from heaven, O Lucifer, son of the morning! How you are cut down to the ground, You who weakened the nations! For you have said in your heart: 'I will ascend into heaven, I will exalt my throne above the stars of God; I will also sit on the mount of the congregation On the farthest sides of the north; I will ascend above the heights of the clouds, I will be like the Most High.'" (Isaiah 14:12-14)

In this last passage from the fourteenth chapter of Isaiah, God once again allows us to know that this is not a fallen angel but a fallen king (man):

Yet you shall be brought down to Sheol, To the lowest
depths of the Pit. "Those who see you will gaze at you, And
consider you, saying: 'Is this the man who made the earth
tremble, Who shook kingdoms, Who made the world as a
wilderness And destroyed its cities, Who did not open the
house of his prisoners?'" (Isaiah 14:15-17)

Like many others, the prideful and boastful king of Babylon learned a
humbling lesson from God. The Bible advises us about humility, "And who-
ever exalts himself will be humbled, and he who humbles himself will be
exalted" (Matthew 23:12).

So He drove out the man; and He placed cherubim at the
east of the garden of Eden, and a flaming sword which
turned every way, to guard the way to the tree of life.
(Genesis 3:24)

Moreover the word of the Lord came to me, saying, "Son
of man, take up a lamentation for the king of Tyre, and say
to him, 'Thus says the Lord GOD: "You were the seal of
perfection, Full of wisdom and perfect in beauty. You were
in Eden, the garden of God; Every precious stone was your
covering: The sardius, topaz, and diamond, Beryl, onyx,
and jasper, Sapphire, turquoise, and emerald with gold. The
workmanship of your timbrels and pipes Was prepared for
you on the day you were created. "You were the anointed
cherub who covers; I established you; You were on the holy
mountain of God; You walked back and forth in the midst
of fiery stones. You were perfect in your ways from the day
you were created, Till iniquity was found in you. "By the
abundance of your trading You became filled with violence
within, And you sinned; Therefore I cast you as a profane
thing Out of the mountain of God; And I destroyed you, O
covering cherub, From the midst of the fiery stones. "Your
heart was lifted up because of your beauty; You corrupted
your wisdom for the sake of your splendor; I cast you to
the ground, I laid you before kings, That they might gaze at
you. (Ezekiel 28:11-17)

In these passages from Ezekiel, the king of Tyre's character is compared to that of one of the beautiful cherubim that was given the authority to protect the tree of life in the Garden of Eden.

With this action taken, cursed Adam and Eve would not have access to it to gain spiritual life again. Unfortunately, one of the free-willed cherubim chose the wicked path to destruction because of its enormous pride for its beauty, but the cherub did not tempt Adam and Eve to eat from the tree of the knowledge of good and evil. These scriptures plainly allow us to understand that the dragon, ancient serpent, or the devil is not the same as the mentioned prideful guardian cherub. Both the dragon and the cherub were once in the Garden of Eden. However, the cherub had a God-given free will and was another creation of God, for His glorious purpose, that failed him. An accurate description of how cherubim look is found in the first and tenth chapters of the book of Ezekiel. Please take note, cherubim are not human babies with wings as some have inaccurately imagined and depicted.

> Do not add to His words, Lest He rebuke you, and you be
> found a liar. (Proverbs 30:6)

Let us always be wise and not add to the flawless word of God. If we don't know something, it's acceptable to just say so. Many inaccuracies have been spoken and written about our enemy, the devil, the ancient serpent, or the dragon, that can't be proved with God's Holy Bible. The most interesting thing about it is that nowhere within the sixty-six books of the Holy Bible can you find that the devil is, or was, an angel of light. However, here are some of the names that he is known by:

-dragon/serpent of old (Revelation 12:9)
-serpent (Genesis 3:1)
-beast of the earth/field (Genesis 1:25)
-Leviathan, king over all the children of pride (Job 41)
-the devil (Matthew 4:1)
-murderer/liar/father of lies (John 8:44)
-Satan (Job 1:6)
-the accuser of our brethren (Revelation 12:10)
-the tempter (Matthew 4:3)
-Beelzebub/ruler of the demons (Matthew 12:24)
-Belial (2 Corinthians 6:15)
-the enemy (Matthew 13:39)
-the wicked one (Matthew 13:19)
-prince of the power of the air (Ephesians 2:2)
-power of darkness (Colossians 1:13)

-the adversary (1 Peter 5:8)
-god of this age/world (2 Corinthians 4:4)
-rulers of the darkness/spiritual hosts of wickedness in the heavenly places
   (Ephesians 6:12)

Again, there is no sentence or phrase indicating that Satan's origin was as an angel of light. The Holy Bible only states that the devil can transform, masquerade, or pretend to be an angel, or messenger of light (2 Corinthians 11:14). God doesn't mention Satan as an angel of light in His word because Satan never was.

God is the absolute expert, and he is beyond wisdom and beyond understanding. No one should feel that it is necessary to add to or take away from His perfect word. The word can defend itself. We all must revere God's word and be accountable for what we say and write about it. God's answers to His revelations are given to us, and it is impossible to solve them without him revealing them to us. Some have decided to add their assumptions, opinions, and thoughts to God's word without revelation knowledge. This has been proved to be very unwise and has confused others. The mischievous and wicked devil thrives and preys on people's ignorance. When this ignorance has combined with the spread of unwise thoughts, opinions, and assumptions through speech and writing, the devil has destroyed many people (Hosea 4:6).

Satan the Accuser and Tempter

> Then the Lord said to Satan, "Have you considered My servant Job, that there is none like him on the earth, a blameless and upright man, one who fears God and shuns evil?" So Satan answered the Lord and said, "Does Job fear God for nothing? Have You not made a hedge around him, around his household, and around all that he has on every side? You have blessed the work of his hands, and his possessions have increased in the land. But now, stretch out Your hand and touch all that he has, and he will surely curse You to Your face!" And the Lord said to Satan, "Behold, all that he has is in your power; only do not lay a hand on his person." So Satan went out from the presence of the Lord. (Job 1:8-12)

Satan's accusations against the people of God are enormous and continual. Like he did to the faithful servant Job, the devil is angrily watching us, and he is always pointing the finger to accuse us. The enemy is always on the prowl to attempt to kill, steal from, and destroy faithful servants of God (John 10:10).

In Job's case, God did give the devil permission to cause havoc in order to prove that Satan's accusations were false. Through all the turmoil that Satan caused, Job remained faithful and did not curse God to His face. God richly restored Job for all of the troubles that he had encountered (Job 42:10-16). Once again, the devil was proved to be a liar. Nonetheless, destructive Satan is relentless, and day and night he uses his poisonous mouth to accuse the saints, here referred to as "brethren," as the book of Revelation shows: "Then

I heard a loud voice saying in heaven, 'Now salvation, and strength, and the kingdom of our God, and the power of His Christ have come, for the accuser of our brethren, who accused them before our God day and night, has been cast down'" (Revelation 12:10).

Satan has been tempting mankind for thousands of years, and he is ruthless. As the spiritual devil tempts Jesus Christ, it becomes obvious in these scriptures that he often uses the word of God to tempt or trick us: "Then the devil took Him up into the holy city, set Him on the pinnacle of the temple, and said to Him, 'If You are the Son of God, throw Yourself down. For it is written:

> "He shall give His angels charge over you," and, "In their hands they shall bear you up, Lest you dash your foot against a stone."' Jesus said to him, 'It is written again, "You shall not tempt the Lord your God"' (Matthew 4:5-7).

Now, Jesus knew that he was being tempted by the prince of the power of the air (Ephesians 2:2). But some of us don't realize that the devil is trying to tempt us because of how crafty he is. Because we can't see the air, he can masterfully manipulate the unsuspecting if he chooses not to appear in an evil spiritual form. The devil, who talks much, has been present for thousands of years, and he knows all of the scriptures, which is another way he masquerades as an angel of God. However, God's sheep should know His voice (John 10:4). Also, we shouldn't be ignorant of Satan's devices (2 Corinthians 2:11). Therefore, we, too, must use the flawless word of God, which is our mighty Spirit's sword (Ephesians 6:17), along with putting on the full armor of God (Ephesians 6:13-16), and do as Jesus did to defeat Satan's seductive temptations. However, the wisest thing to do is not to have a conversation with the devil at all because he can out-con the world's greatest con artist. We must all remember that death soon followed for Eve and Adam when Eve conversed with Satan!

The spiritual devil, which was once a physical wild beast of the field, tempts Jesus Christ among his origin, other wild beasts, in the wilderness:

> Immediately the Spirit drove Him into the wilderness. And He was there in the wilderness forty days, tempted by Satan, and was with the wild beasts; and the angels ministered to Him. (Mark 1:12-13)

Satan The Destroyer

This charge I commit to you, son Timothy, according to the prophecies previously made concerning you, that by them you may wage the good warfare, having faith and a good conscience, which some having rejected, concerning the faith have suffered shipwreck, of whom are Hymenaeus and Alexander, whom I delivered to Satan that they may learn not to blaspheme. (1 Timothy 1:18-20)

It is actually reported that there is sexual immorality among you, and such sexual immorality as is not even named among the Gentiles—that a man has his father's wife! And you are puffed up, and have not rather mourned, that he who has done this deed might be taken away from among you. For I indeed, as absent in body but present in spirit, have already judged (as though I were present) him who has so done this deed. In the name of our Lord Jesus Christ, when you are gathered together, along with my spirit, with the power of our Lord Jesus Christ, deliver such a one to Satan for the destruction of the flesh, that his spirit may be saved in the day of the Lord Jesus. (1 Corinthians 5:1-5)

In these passages, it shows us that God also uses the devil to control, restrain, or correct the evil desires of people. God, who chastises those he loves (Hebrews 12:6), has various ways that he corrects us. We should be thankful that God would love us enough to discipline us by His wisdom, according to what he determines is best.

The Snake (New Serpent) Lies under Your Feet!

And the Lord God said to the woman, "What is this you have done?" The woman said, "The serpent deceived me, and I ate." (Genesis 3:13)

And I will put enmity Between you and the woman, And between your seed and her Seed; He shall bruise your head, And you shall bruise his heel." (Genesis 3:15)

Who is the serpent's seed? The serpent does have seed, or offspring, as does Eve. The serpent's offspring are other serpents. Eve's offspring are people. Some people who first see a snake want to kill it even though it is low to the ground. The reason for this is that we are all connected to the original betrayal in Genesis and the curse of enmity that God placed on the serpent. The physical and spiritual snakes have the ability to strike our heels, in other words, to inflict pain. Some physical serpents have killed people, and we know the spiritual serpent has killed people. For example, Satan treacherously killed Job's children in the first chapter of the book of Job. We must keep the spiritual serpent under our feet by continually crushing his head!

Some snakes have the ability to glide in the air from tree to tree. This limited flight is a reminder that the serpent in its original form, with wings, flew before God cursed it. The answer that many are seeking, by digging in the ground for dinosaur fossils, can be found by researching the snake. By researching and studying the new serpent, information can be discovered about the dragon. The Deoxyribonucleic acid (DNA) of snakes needs to be studied and researched further, along with the dragons' fossils DNA, because they will match. By doing this, it will be concrete evidence that they are synonymous.

There once lived a well-known and enormous sea serpent named Leviathan that was recorded in the holy scriptures. The cursed Leviathan dragon once moved along with the ships of the sea. The enormous Leviathan serpent was later destroyed by God. An accurate description of the Leviathan serpent is found in the forty-first chapter of Job. Also, the Leviathan dragon is mentioned in these holy scriptures:

> There the ships sail about; there is that Leviathan Which You have made to play there. (Psalm 104:26)

> In that day the Lord with His severe sword, great and strong, Will punish Leviathan the fleeing serpent, Leviathan that twisted serpent; And He will slay the reptile that is in the sea. (Isaiah 27:1)

> You broke the heads of Leviathan in pieces, And gave him as food to the people inhabiting the wilderness. (Psalm 74:14)

The Big Lie about Evolution and Dinosaurs

In the beginning God created the heavens and the earth. (Genesis 1:1)

He has made the earth by His power, He has established the world by His wisdom, And has stretched out the heavens at His discretion. (Jeremiah 10:12)

The devil and man's influence of lies have brought forth counterfeits of God's Creation account, which are the evolution theory, the Big Bang theory, and theistic evolution. The evolution theory, which is not a fact, unsuccessfully tries to eliminate God's role in creating us. The Big Bang theory is usually defined as a random explosive event that created the universe, and theistic evolution, which includes long-age evolutionary theories, states that the explosive Big Bang was directed by God.

Now, the lies that contradict God's Genesis account, which have been told for many years, will fall to Creation. There is no coincidence that the deceitful dragon's fossils are associated with the misleading evolution theory. The fall was great for the deceitful dragon, and the fall will be great for the deceitful evolution theory!

Without a doubt, God created us, the earth, and the heavens. Why is it that some people doubt what God can do, when we witness all of His vast creations, including people, around us everyday? Shouldn't God be given praise and glory for His marvelous creations from everyone one of us? It is

43

sad to know that some people don't want to give God honor for creating us in His wonderful image. The Creator God will never be proved a liar. God did create us, the earth, and the heavens!

The dinosaur name will vanish because it never existed, and it was not here millions of years ago! Evolution, which includes the dinosaur findings and has a great deal to do with it, has an end of destruction because of the many fabricated and unstable pieces of information within it. One of these pieces of information is, the controversy surroundings the reason for dinosaurs' extinction, and scientists have no clear answer. Also, some scientists falsely state that dinosaurs evolved into birds. The only solution to evolution is simple: God is science. He has vast understanding and knowledge of all things to the smallest degree. It is very important to God that we know he created us with His very own hands, and that we are not here by chance or by evolving, but by the love and pleasure of God's own perfect will. God's Creation is stable, unlike the evolution theory, and God's truth about Creation will never change. As the Bible tells us, "I will praise You, for I am fearfully and wonderfully made; Marvelous are Your works, And that my soul knows very well" (Psalm 139:14). Also, "having a form of godliness but denying its power. And from such people turn away!" (2 Timothy 3:5).

While taking biology classes in high school and college, I often thought about evolution versus Creation. Because I am a Christian, I couldn't swallow the information about evolution. To be told that we as humans evolved to be better forms of apes is very insulting. Some say that because they hate the image of God and would prefer to say that they evolved from an image of an ape instead of the wonderful and glorious image of God. Also, if we evolved from apes, why are apes still here? (I know the answer that is given, but it still doesn't make rational sense to me). If we are evolving into better adapted human bodies, why are our life spans shorter than many of those people in biblical records who lived long ago? God allows us to know that he shortened our life spans to be no more than 120 years (Genesis 6:3). There are very few people, of the billions of people currently living, who will live to be 120 years old.

Why should evolution have its say, and influence so many young people in schools? Shouldn't creationism be given a voice for the youth in all schools? I never accepted that we as humans are the products of evolution because, we are too complex and so well designed. God's creation of me is the only reason for my existence on earth. God is self-sufficient and lacks nothing, and I feel privileged that he would think so much of me to create me in His own wonderful image.

There is no coincidence that the deceptive dragon's fossils are the main force behind evolution, which attempts and fails to destroy creationism. Yes, the devil's bones are the main source that fuels the evolution theory. Evolution has too many dead-end roads, because it is a set of assumptions that have not been proved to be facts. Creation is an open highway which includes man's history. There are no pre-historic times, we are history. Any time before Adam and Eve was God, who is the beginning.

Many of us in those biology classes believed in God, but we had to have evolution thrown at us like a fast ball. Like a fast ball, evolution is hard to see, and when we thought that we could see it, it passed us, and we ended up striking out! It is time for God's truth about Creation to have a chance to bat in all schools. The youth will hit a home run with God's Creation!

4

Understanding God's Ways

Why Did It Happen?

But our God is in heaven; He does whatever He pleases. (Psalm 115:3)

I form the light and create darkness: I make peace, and create evil; I the Lord do all these things. (Isaiah 45:7) —King James Version

All things were made through Him, and without Him nothing was made that was made. (John 1:3)

Does not the potter have power over the clay, from the same lump to make one vessel for honor and another for dishonor? What if God, wanting to show His wrath and to make His power known, endured with much longsuffering the vessels of wrath prepared for destruction, and that He might make known the riches of His glory on the vessels of mercy, which He had prepared beforehand for glory, even us whom He called, not of the Jews only, but also of the Gentiles? (Romans 9:21-24)

In the first chapter of the book of Genesis, God describes His Creations as "good" or "very good," but not as "perfect." Before God cursed man and animal, the old serpent had already proved to be untrustworthy by lying to Eve about the tree of knowledge, saying that death would not come to Adam and her if they ate from it. God made everything for either an honorable or a dishonorable purpose. The devil was created for a dishonorable purpose. God cursed the dragon, who he made crafty, and Satan will be tormented forever in the lake of brimstone and fire. God's will has been and will be done.

Please take note again: the devil was already evil and a liar before man knew of good and evil. It was only after they ate from the forbidden tree that Adam and Eve realized what good and evil were. Their innocent eyes were only then opened to know the difference between good and evil, but the devil was created to be evil and a murderer from his beginning. God created the devil, who is evil; therefore, God created evil. God, who created both, knows the difference between good and evil (Genesis 3:22), but God, who has his own will, only chooses to do good.

You may ponder why God put a tree in the Garden of Eden that he didn't want Adam and Eve to eat from. God is sovereign and he is a tester. He is always testing us and through God wanting Adam and Eve to fail, they, as well as us, are able to learn more about who he is, which allows us to learn from our failures. The devil is a tempter, and it is important for us to know who God is by His holy ways. Because God can't lie, he had to create the lying, crafty devil to tempt man. As many know, the master potter is God, and the devil was made for a dishonorable purpose to attempt to deceive mankind, which he did, and he continues to do. Adam and Eve made a choice to listen to the devil, or dragon, who had no free will, and they disobeyed God's command and ate from the forbidden tree. Like Adam and Eve, we, too, are being tested and tempted, and our God-given free will allows us to choose between good and evil.

> Yet Michael the archangel, in contending with the devil, when he disputed about the body of Moses, dared not bring against him a reviling accusation, but said, "The Lord rebuke you!" But these speak evil of whatever they do not know; and whatever they know naturally, like brute beasts, in these things they corrupt themselves. (Jude 1: 9-10)

In these two verses from the book of Jude, Michael, the archangel, did not bring accusations against the devil over Moses' body because he understands why Satan was created. Why bother accusing a liar who has no choice but to be one? It would have been irrational for Michael to waste time accusing the devil. For this reason, we should not accuse the devil. We should always rebuke the devil, and we should be wise to never have a conversation with him or follow his evil ways! We must always "therefore submit to God. Resist the devil and he will flee from you" (James 4:7).

The only way to be obedient to God is to have a reverential fear of him (Psalm 89:7). We all have choices to make. Our God-given free will needs to be used wisely. God molded us, but our wills determine our inevitable fate. God's ways are holy, upright, fair, and just. God's plans are perfect. His will is the final say, and what has happened is how unique God is in His immortal ways. The purpose for our existence is to praise, obey, and have reverential fear of God. It is not about me or you, it is about God. It always has been and it always will be about God. No one takes precedent over God. It is God's plan that we know who he is. God knows who we are; he has known us from the beginning of time, before we knew ourselves. We are here because God loves us and for His own pleasure.

> The devil, who deceived them, was cast into the lake of fire
> and brimstone where the beast and the false prophet are.
> And they will be tormented day and night forever and ever.
> (Revelation 20:10)

The crafty devil's final, inevitable fate will be to be thrown into the lake of fire and brimstone, and to be tormented forever. In the end, God will have no further use for the deceitful and murderous devil. He will be cast away from the presence of God and His people, who will inherit eternal life and peace on the new earth (Revelation 21:1). On God's new earth, the imperfections and curses that we suffer from will be no more (Revelation 22:3). What an exciting time that will be!

Understanding the Spirits of Man and Animal

> All go to one place: all are from the dust, and all return to dust. Who knows the spirit of the sons of men, which goes upward, and the spirit of the animal, which goes down to the earth? (Ecclesiastes 3:20-21)

> Remember your Creator before the silver cord is loosed, Or the golden bowl is broken, Or the pitcher shattered at the fountain, Or the wheel broken at the well. Then the dust will return to the earth as it was, And the spirit will return to God who gave it. (Ecclesiastes 12:6-7)

From wise King Solomon comes a very thought-provoking question in the first quote from Ecclesiastes, and God knows the answer. Where does the flesh of men and animals go? The flesh of both men and animals came from the dust, so they both go back to the dust. Where do the spirits of men and animals go? The spirits of animals, which make them living beings, remain on earth after their flesh goes back to the dust. However, the spirits of humans go up to God. Ecclesiastes 12:6-7 says specifically that a man's spirit returns to God because man's spirit came from God. God breathed into the nostrils of man, which made him a living being: "And the Lord God formed man of the dust of the ground, and breathed into his nostrils the breath of life; and man became a living being" (Genesis 2:7).

Along with God's explanation that animals' spirits stay on the earth after they die, God's word also has information about evil or demonic spirits. The Satanic spirits of serpents, scorpions, spiders, and other powers of the enemy can multiply because they are always physically dying. They also appear in heaven and can visit third heaven. The books of Job, Ephesians, and Mark show us these abilities :

> Now there was a day when the sons of God came to present themselves before the Lord, and Satan also came among them. (Job 1:6)

> For we do not wrestle against flesh and blood, but against principalities, against powers, against the rulers of the darkness of this age, against spiritual hosts of wickedness in the heavenly places. (Ephesians 6:12)

> For He said to him, "Come out of the man, unclean spirit!" Then He asked him, "What is your name?" And he answered, saying, "My name is Legion; for we are many." (Mark 5:8-9)

Jesus speaks the truth to inform us that we have the authority to trample on or crush serpents, scorpions, and all powers of the enemy (Luke 10:19). The cursed physical serpents' minds are not like the spiritual serpents' minds. The spiritual serpents' minds are advanced and wicked. Following the physical animals' curse, they can't talk, nor can they be crafty and deceive us. However, when animals die, their spirits become crafty again, and they regain the ability to talk. An example of the serpent's wicked and advanced spiritual mind is when Satan tempts Jesus Christ in Matthew chapter 4, which was discussed earlier. With the advanced minds of the spiritual demons named Legion, they begged Jesus to cast them into pigs, which were physical animals, similar to what they used to be (Mark 5:11-13). Also, other examples of evil spirits that were created by God from their beginning, not from the dust but from heaven, are found in 1 Samuel 16:14 and 1 Kings 22:22-23.

Many things of the spiritual realm are unknown, and even things on the physical earth, where we currently live, are unknown. Because our thinking is earthly, the spiritual realm can only be understood through the guidance of the Holy Spirit. As Jesus says, "However, when He, the Spirit of truth, has come, He will guide you into all truth; for He will not speak on His own authority, but whatever He hears He will speak; and He will tell you things to come" (John 16:13).

Now, our souls are different from our spirits. Our souls are part of our God-given free wills. With our God-given free wills, we can choose to love and serve God (Mark 12:30). The Holy Bible never states that animals have souls, which confirms that animals don't have a God-given free will, as explained earlier about the serpent. God can separate our spirits from our souls (Hebrews 4:12). Jesus Christ wisely tells us that we can choose to either save or lose our souls because of our God-given free choice:

> "For whoever desires to save his life will lose it, but whoever loses his life for My sake will find it. For what profit is it to a man if he gains the whole world, and loses his own soul? Or what will a man give in exchange for his soul? For the Son of Man will come in the glory of His Father with His angels, and then He will reward each according to his works" (Matthew 16:25-27).

God's Timing: Right Time and Right Season to Be Revealed

> To everything there is a season, A time for every purpose under heaven. (Ecclesiastes 3:1)

God's timing is perfect. Now is God's pre-determined season for this awesome truth to come forth. There is always a due season for God to make the unexplainable explainable. God's patience can't be fathomed. It amazes me how God sees and hears untrue things, but His patience allows him to wait until the appointed time he has called to give a revelation. God has allowed so much to be built up about the fictitious dinosaur and the false identity of the devil, knowing these fictions would be destroyed and would come tumbling down. The misinformation that is available about the dinosaur creature and the devil is enormous; and there are so many speculations, which have brought out many untruths. God is bigger than any myth or lie! God comes forth and opens my eyes to see what no man could imagine: that the snake is the dragon and the devil.

God explains natural phenomena because God is science. God makes the impossible possible. God is a God of miracles. God specializes in showing mankind that he does things that make us ask, "How?" Now is the perfect time for God to show the reason for what has been revealed. The towering evolution theory will be destroyed, just like the Tower of Babel in the Old Testament. God allows, watches, and then says, "Time is up, and now let me show man that I have heard and seen enough, and only my power will be left standing." During the building of the Tower of Babel, he gave people many languages to stop them. With the answer to the mythical dinosaur, he will change some men's hearts and their minds about this made-up creature that is a part of evolution. God can patiently watch, and then quickly destroy those things that need to come to an end. God is the Omega, the End of all things (Revelation 22:13).

By reading the book of Revelation, you will come to an understanding that the earth will come to a destructive end. God will bring an end to an evil and prideful world that has built itself up. With that being said, you always come from what he has done or will do with total reverence. Because, no one can do things the way that God does things, he gets your attention. He is God, and there is no other.

5

God: The Source of Solutions

No Missing Pieces: The Puzzle Is Complete

> He uncovers deep things out of darkness, And brings the shadow of death to light. (Job 12:22)

The great mystery has been revealed once and for all! The snake, dragon, devil, Satan, and the mythical dinosaur are all the same. All of the pieces to the puzzle are in place, and they fit together perfectly. God sometimes gives bits and pieces of a puzzle over time, which ultimately come together to bring forth understanding and knowledge. Some revelations are coming forth now, because we are approaching a time of solved mysteries. God's mysteries can't be solved without His assistance. God reveals answers when he is ready. Many will read this and believe, and some won't, but what has been written is the godly truth. The fossils that have been left behind, the evidence, does show what God has told the world about the dragon, or ancient serpent. God makes the unknown known. No one should ever doubt what Almighty God can do! God is not the author of confusion, but the author of solutions.

> Lead me in Your truth and teach me, For You are the God of my salvation; On You I wait all the day. (Psalm 25:5)

> And He opened their understanding, that they might comprehend the Scriptures. (Luke 24:45)

It is my hope and prayer that God will open many people's eyes so they can understand this great revelation of the true identity of the spiritual devil, which was but an animal created from dust on the sixth day. When God opens our minds to see the truth, he opens the door for us to better understand His eternal purpose and plan. Adam and Eve, like us, had free will. God created a physical animal that tempted our original parents, and they chose to listen. We, too, are being tempted by the spiritual devil. But, the gift of eternal life is available to us if we choose Jesus Christ (John 3:16).

God Is Truth!

That by two immutable things, in which it is impossible for God to lie, we might have strong consolation, who have fled for refuge to lay hold of the hope set before us. (Hebrews 6:18)

It is impossible for God to lie, and there is no reason for God to lie. He can do anything. If he speaks something, it will be done. With no limits, what is too hard for God to do? He created the heavens and the earth, and he created all living things. God is truth, and he is victory! If God said that he cursed the dragon or serpent, then that is what he did. It wasn't complicated for God. Is anything too complicated for God to do? No matter what passage you read in the Holy Bible, the inevitable is, God is truth! Those who serve God know that he will never lie! Because we know that, we should always be on His team of truth and be greatly encouraged!

The enormous lies that surround the dinosaurs, the evolution theory, and the origin of the devil have become Goliaths. However, like David, who struck down one Goliath with a rock, a sling shot, and God's help, God will again use His power to tear down these Goliaths (1 Samuel 17:48-51). So, when these Goliaths fall and the dust settles, God will be standing with His truth!

God Can Do Anything!

For with God nothing will be impossible. (Luke 1:37)

God makes the impossible possible. I don't understand God's power, I just know that His power is infinite. When God revealed this mystery to me, I knew that he was giving this to me to tell the world at the proper time. I never want to question what God can do, I just know that he can do all things. Yes, I have read some articles on the dinosaur, and with no doubt, I knew that God cursed the true animal, the dragon, when he gave me the revelation. Those who wrote and spoke in error about the dinosaur didn't know, simply because God didn't tell them. God's knowledge and understanding makes all the difference. People come and go, but God remains. He knows all of the deep secrets, and they are His to share when he wants to share them.

God wants each of us to know the truth, and he has made it possible. With this book, I have pleased God. That will always be my only goal: to please him first through my acts of obedience. I walk by faith and not by sight (2 Corinthians 5:7) because I know that God is always in control. God created the devil, ancient serpent, or dragon on the sixth day and cursed it. The animal that we know as the snake is not dead or extinct, but is still alive and roams the earth! During the great flood, he kept the dragon's fossils safe from harm, for His divine purpose. God, who speaks things into existence, with the sound of His voice, commands awesome things to happen. God makes no mistakes, and His limitless power and intelligence allows him to do whatever he pleases.

The Divine Plan of God

> For God so loved the world that He gave His only begotten
> Son, that whoever believes in Him should not perish but
> have everlasting life. (John 3:16)

God allowed the dragon or serpent to tempt our original parents, but he
also allows us to be redeemed because he tremendously loves us. God's plan
of redemption through His only begotten son, Jesus Christ, is the ultimate
design of divine perfection. The first man, Adam, came from the dust and
sinned, but Jesus, who is from heaven and is sinless, came to redeem us all
from our sins. God foreknew that Adam and Eve would disobey him. Therefore the Lamb, Jesus Christ, was slain or crucified from the beginning of the
world (Revelation 13:8).

> And so it is written, "The first man Adam became a living
> being." The last Adam became a life-giving spirit. However,
> the spiritual is not first, but the natural, and afterward the
> spiritual. The first man was of the earth, made of dust; the
> second Man is the Lord from heaven. As was the man of
> dust, so also are those who are made of dust; and as is the
> heavenly Man, so also are those who are heavenly. And as we
> have borne the image of the man of dust, we shall also bear
> the image of the heavenly Man. (1 Corinthians 15: 45-49)

There is a greater place than the Garden of Eden, and it is called the Kingdom
of God, which many people will inherit for eternity. This is the new life that
many will live. The Garden of Eden was "very good," but the new earth will

be perfect. There are differences between something very good and something perfect. The knowledge of good and evil entered the world through disobedience, but through Jesus' act of obedience we all can have eternal life. So, the plan of redemption is perfect just as God knew it would be.

> Now I saw a new heaven and a new earth, for the first heaven and the first earth had passed away. Also there was no more sea. Then I, John, saw the holy city, New Jerusalem, coming down out of heaven from God, prepared as a bride adorned for her husband. And I heard a loud voice from heaven saying, "Behold, the tabernacle of God is with men, and He will dwell with them, and they shall be His people. God Himself will be with them and be their God. And God will wipe away every tear from their eyes; there shall be no more death, nor sorrow, nor crying. There shall be no more pain, for the former things have passed away." Then He who sat on the throne said, "Behold, I make all things new." And He said to me, "Write, for these words are true and faithful." (Revelation 21:1-5)

God will destroy this earth and create a new earth, because that is what he wants to do. God's will dominates all. Also, God wisely tells us through the Prophet Isaiah that animals will not hurt or destroy in the new earth. The serpent, which will eat dust, will be in the newly created earth, but this is not the spiritual devil of the first earth.

> For behold, I create new heavens and a new earth; And the former shall not be remembered or come to mind. (Isaiah 65:17)

> The wolf and the lamb shall feed together, The lion shall eat straw like the ox, And dust shall be the serpent's food. They shall not hurt nor destroy in all My holy mountain," says the Lord. (Isaiah 65:25)

Conclusion

> The fear of the Lord is the beginning of wisdom, And the knowledge of the Holy One is understanding. (Proverbs 9:10)

Many things have been taught to me, a reverential and fearful servant of the Lord, that have not been taught to me by people, but by God, who is the Master Teacher. No one can out-teach all-knowing God. I am still learning, and I will continue to learn from God with an obedient heart. I am both humbled and honored to be an eternal student of the Lord.

With this insightful truth, I have learned that some things begin and end in similar ways. God allows some things in history to repeat themselves. For example, a deceitful dragon, an animal, in Genesis lied to Adam and Eve. In the end, in the book of Revelation, two beasts, also animals, will deceive many people. In the second and third chapters of Genesis, the tree of life is present, and in the twenty-second chapter of Revelation, the tree of life is once again present. King Solomon's words are true that there is nothing new under the sun: "That which has been is what will be, That which is done is what will be done, And there is nothing new under the sun. Is there anything of which it may be said, 'See, this is new'? It has already been in ancient times before us" (Ecclesiastes 1:9-10).

It is my prayer and expectation that, as I journey with this truth, I will be able to continue as a vessel of God who simply wants to help and encourage those who are presently in the Body of Christ. I also want to draw others who are not yet in the Body to Jesus Christ. As the Bible tells us, "The fruit of the righteous is a tree of life, And he who wins souls is wise" (Proverbs 11:30).

> Then the Lord answered me and said: "Write the vision and make it plain on tablets, That he may run who reads it." (Habakkuk 2:2)

God's will was to make this profound truth plain and simple, and to give it to the world. It is not a concern of mine that some will reject this truth, that God has so freely given to me. My goal is to always appease and please God. Some reject Jesus Christ, who is the only way to God's salvation. Therefore, I will not fret when those who are doubtful or in disbelief say things against what is the God-given truth and what is written in the Holy Bible. The truth will always remain.

God gave me this truth to tell to the world because that is what God wants to do at this time. The Holy Bible wisely tells us how God chooses people to use with these faithful scriptures:

> But God has chosen the foolish things of the world to put to shame the wise, and God has chosen the weak things of the world to put to shame the things which are mighty; and the base things of the world and the things which are despised God has chosen, and the things which are not, to bring to nothing the things that are, that no flesh should glory in His presence. (1 Corinthians 1: 27-29)

The devil put a thorn in the apostle Paul's side to keep him from becoming conceited when Paul was given great and surpassing revelations (2 Corinthians 12:7). I, too, have been spiritually attacked for knowing this revelation of the true identity of Satan, the cursed dragon, and for knowing other revelations. But to God be the glory, and no weapon forged against me by the devil has prospered or will prosper (Isaiah 54:17)!

God wants us to know that our primary enemies are nothing more than cursed dragons, which lost their original forms, and now are simply lowly snakes that were created on the sixth day, like us, from the dust. Once they die, their Satanic and demonic spirits can roam the earth and the heavens until they are thrown into the lake of brimstone and fire. As stated before, the wicked devil and his demons are very knowledgeable about the Holy Bible. They know that their time is short, and that their inevitable fate is to be eternally tormented. They tremble at God: "You believe that there is one God. You do well. Even the demons believe and tremble!" (James 2:19).

With this profound truth from God, barriers will be broken in our minds to help us and strengthen us to understand that since the beginning, we have had dominion, through Christ Jesus to overcome and conquer Satan, his demons, and his powers. When we know Satan's true origin, we are no longer a slave to a lie, but are set free with the absolute truth! "Therefore if the Son makes you free, you shall be free indeed" (John 8:36).

Printed in the United States
131480LV00002B/21/P